T0077897

BOOK

of

SERMONS

MARVIN WATSON

authorHOUSE®

AuthorHouse™
1663 Liberty Drive
Bloomington, IN 47403
www.authorhouse.com
Phone: 833-262-8899

Published by AuthorHouse 09/14/2020

ISBN: 978-1-7283-7338-6 (sc)
ISBN: 978-1-7283-7337-9 (e)

Library of Congress Control Number: 2020917436

Print information available on the last page.

Any people depicted in stock imagery provided by Getty Images are models,
and such images are being used for illustrative purposes only.
Certain stock imagery © Getty Images.

This book is printed on acid-free paper.

Because of the dynamic nature of the Internet, any web addresses or links contained in
this book may have changed since publication and may no longer be valid. The views
expressed in this work are solely those of the author and do not necessarily reflect the
views of the publisher, and the publisher hereby disclaims any responsibility for them.

Scripture taken from the King James Version of the Bible.

Scripture quotations marked NLT are taken from the Holy Bible, New Living Translation,
copyright © 1996, 2004, 2015 by Tyndale House Foundation. Used by permission of
Tyndale House Publishers, Inc., Carol Stream, Illinois 60188. All rights reserved.

CONTENTS

INTRODUCTION

The sermons I have included in this book capture a certain situation that all of us will have to deal with at one time or another. I allowed God to use me and talk to me as I began to write.

What I thought about the most as I was writing is what the world is going through today, and how can they be most helped in today's climate of challenges. I took into consideration who my audience is and what I am going through. Chances are if I am going through something, someone else must be going through something too.

We will always have to deal with the devil's tricks, challenges, and difficulties. These are all designed to take you off the mark God has set in motion for your life. The devil also wants you to not only lose faith in yourself, but in God as well. Just because something you have been waiting for doesn't come when you think it should, or God doesn't seem to answer your prayers exactly when you want Him to, does not mean He isn't going to answer your prayers.

There is a powerful word about what I was just talking about and that is: *"Godliness with contentment is great gain"* (I Tim. 6:6) (KJV). In other words, we must have patience. We must have patience in dealing with ourselves, our fellowman as well as God Himself. After all, He has patience with us, so why shouldn't we have patience with someone else or each other?

One of the things I tried to express in this book is not only having discipline but boldness in dealing with the devil and his people. There are times when some people align their lives with the devil himself. They try to block your progress, make your life miserable, and see you fall if possible. You just have to know who you are in Christ and develop a thick skin when dealing with problems or situations that you would rather not have to deal with at all.

What I also tried to make certain of is the fact that, *"All that shall live Godly in Christ Jesus will suffer persecution"*. **(II Tim. 3:12** (KJV) The Apostle Paul talked about it. Jesus talked about it and this book talks about this too.

May you be richly blessed as you read, take notes, underline or highlight your favorite passages of Scripture, or favorite sermons that can be of the most help to you. I would also hope you would not keep it to yourself but share it with friends, relatives, or give it away as a gift to someone less fortunate than yourself.

Thank you so much for getting and reading this book.

CHAPTER 1

WHY WE NEED THE
FRUIT OF THE SPIRIT

As believers, we need the fruit of the Spirit because they help us deal with our fellowman in a genuine, peaceful, and loving manner. I am going to explain each fruit and tell you why it is important.

The first quality a Christian should possess is love as stated in (Gal. 5:22) (KJV) and Jn. 13:34-35, (KJV). A Christian's life should also be marked by joy, which is being cheerful, calm, delightful, and full of gladness even when bad things are happening around you.

For example, bills are due and you don't know where money will come from to pay them. Common sense would dictate that you get upset and begin worrying which will quickly age you. But God says: *"Such love has no fear, because perfect love expels all fear. If we are afraid, it is for fear of punishment, and this shows that we have not fully experienced his perfect love"* (I Jn. 4:18) (NLT). This means you are to love God more than your problems or difficulties.

Next is peace. The Word of God says: *"God will keep you in perfect peace whose mind is stayed on thee because he trusts in thee"* (Is. 26:3) (KJV).

Therefore, if you say you trust in God but have no peace, you are being fooled by the devil. If God's Word says it, that is all that needs to be said because it is impossible for God to lie (Num. 23:19) (KJV).

Christians should also exhibit longsuffering. This means we may have to put up with things or people we don't like. For example, Jesus had to put up with the religious leaders of His day who were constantly trying to find something wrong with Him and what He said. (Mt. 9:10-13) talks about how God is looking for those who need to be healed and delivered from something. As a believer, you should not be concerned about how people talk about you when you minister to prostitutes, drug addicts, sinners or people struggling with something.

However, the religious leaders in the Bible couldn't see it that way. All they could do was act self-righteously and point out what's wrong. Paul was constantly attacked and ridiculed by others. Paul explained to the Corinthians how he went through much suffering for the furtherance of the gospel, (II Cor. 11:22-27).

The next quality we need as Christians is kindness. This simply means to be good to others without expecting anything in return. It also means genuine love for the brethren. An example of this is found in (Rm. 9:1-3), where Paul loved his own people, the Jews, so much that he would rather be without his hope in Christ than to see his own people lost.

Goodness is another quality Christians must have. This simply means showing virtue to someone else just as God does for us (Ps. 27:13). This means when things are not going well, God reaches out and shows goodness so you don't lose heart or give up. An example of this is found in (Jud. 7:9-15).

God said that without faith, it is impossible to please Him (Heb. 11:6) (KJV), so Christians must have faithfulness. Faith is how we get healed (Mt. 17:20). This Scripture is for any problem you need to be delivered from. You may have a mountain of debt, or need healing from some disease or illness, or addicted to drugs and alcohol. Faith is how we hear from God, (Ps. 4:3), how we receive salvation (Eph. 2:8-9), and how we will one day see God (I Thess. 4:16-17).

The life of a Christian should also be marked by gentleness (Gal. 6:1). Essentially, you should restore a person taken by sin in a spirit of meekness or gentleness. This means you should be careful how you speak so as not to make them feel foolish or upset. The Living Bible says: *"and be careful how you approach this person so as not to fall into the same temptation yourself."* (NLT).

The final quality I want to deal with is self-control. This is when someone gives you a reason to strike out at them but you show patience in dealing with them. For example, if a person speaks evil of you or talks about you because of your faith in Christ, you should rejoice because great is your reward in heaven (Mt. 5:10-12). You should also be quick to forgive (Mt. 5:38-40).

TO WHOM WILL YOU SERVE

This is a question that you as a Christian should ask yourself every single day. To whom am I really serving? Are you serving yourself, other gods, other people or even money. If any of these things are your gods than you are not serving the Lord God.

God said in his Word "that all other gods are merely idols, but the Lord made the heavens", **(Ps. 96:4-5)** (KJV). When you serve something or someone, you are loyal to them, and do what it is they want you to do, and you don't let anything else take its' place.

Let's begin with the first humans that were on the earth. God told the man to tend and watch over the Garden of Eden; **(Gen. 2:16)**. After God told him to do that, he also told him to keep away from the "tree of the knowledge of good and evil." Then he not only told them not to do it but why they should not eat of this tree;

(Gen. 2:17).

Now if Adam was a true servant of the Lord and wanted to serve the Lord, he would not have listened to the woman and did the very thing that God told him not to do; **(Gen. 3:6)**. When God saw that they weren't prepared to do what he told Adam to do without question, he had to reject them from being in the garden. This is why he passed judgement on them and also sent them out of the garden. This is found in **(Gen. 3:14)**; **(Gen. 3:16-19)**. Finally, he sent an angel to guard the tree of life, and send them away,

(Gen. 3:23-24).

This is the first example of a situation in which a man did not want to follow and serve the Lord any longer, but instead, took his eyes off the Lord, listened to the woman and died spiritually.

In Moses's day, there was a family of people that followed Moses through the wilderness, but questioned Moses's authority over them and refused to listen or follow Moses any longer. God gave all of the other people a decision to make. This can be found in

(Num. 16:28-33).

It should be pointed out by this last series of scriptures, that when someone tells you something to do and they have the rule over you, it is best that you do what they tell you to do. Otherwise, there will be punishable corrections to be made.

I will give one other example of this from the old testament. This concerns Solomon. Solomon was the son of David, the king, and he warned Solomon not to do anything that would cause God to get mad at him and leave him; **(I Ki. 2:1-4)**. Later on, in Solomon's reign, he asked God for wisdom; **(I Ki. 3:9)**. Then in the next verse, God has something to tell Solomon; **(I Ki. 3:10-14)**.

As Solomon got old, he began marring all of these foreign wives that God told him not to do; which would ultimately cause Solomon to leave the Lord and begin following all of these foreign god's **(I Ki. 11:4-6)**. Then going further, for this is not all that happened as a result of Solomon not serving the Lord, which even he had to make a decision of whom he would serve; **(I Ki. 11:9-12)**.

Again, I ask the question: *"to whom will you serve?"*

Now I want to go to **Deut. 28**, where God gives you a choice; either choose to be blessed or choose curses. In other words, it is not up to God as to whether you get blessed or not, but it is up to you and only you, whether you get cursed or not.

Let's start at **(Deut. 28:1-2)**. This first set of scriptures is telling us that if you fully obey the Lord your God, that all of these other things the scriptures mention is yours.

Once again you must decide to whom are you going to serve. This is what God is asking the nation of Israel. To sweeten the deal, God is telling them that if you do these things God will do all of the good things that he has planned for you.

Some of these things include, verses **(3)** through **(6)**. It is interesting to note that the things God mentions first are all of the things that will bring wealth to you; including your family, seed, herds and so forth. After God gets through talking about this, he then begins to talk about your enemies and how he will protect you from them; **(7)**.

Next God promises those who follow him and do what he has told you to do, will experience more than enough in their cattle, grain as well as the land he is given them **(8)**.

God is not just doing it to those that lived back at that time, but is also telling us that if you do and be what he wants you to be, he will allow you to be blessed so that everyone can see it. In other words, the way you walk and the way you talk and what you have, will tell others that you are the blessed of the Lord; **(9)**.

When people see that you are the blessed of the Lord, they will not mess with you. The first place this can be found in is:

(Gen. 12:10-13); then go down to: **(Gen. 12:16-19)**. So as you can see, even though Abram was scared, God still blessed him and kept anyone, even the king of Egypt, from having Sarai, Abram's wife. God literally sent out from His throne, a consuming fire to terrorize both Pharaoh and his men.

You may be asking yourself, why is God doing this for this person? It is simply because Abraham not only honored and worshiped God, but also used his faith. Ever since God called Abraham, Abraham was faithful to do everything that God told him to do, **(Gen 12:1-3)**.

Another example of this, which is very similar to this one, can be found in **(Gen. 20:1-3)**. Basically what this is saying is that Abraham came to a number of different places where he finally picked out one to settle in. While there, he told this person that this was his sister. This was a little hick-up in Abraham's relationship but God looked at the heart and knew why Abraham did this.

But before this king could lay with her, God appeared to him in a dream and told him that he would kill him for doing this; that she was already married. This is one of the most important parts of this whole story of how God will not only bless you, but protect you as well. He will literally send out his shield of protection to keep you from all hurt, harm and danger. This can be illustrated in, **(Ps. 105:15)**.

This whole subject is called "To Whom Will You Serve?" So far in Abraham's life, this is all he has been doing. That is why God told him that through you, all of the people will be blessed, **(Gen. 22:18)** (NLT). This is only fair since I have been spending a lot of time on people that have not been serving the Lord all of the way.

Let's now go to the new testament to see what people have been doing in some of these same situations. Before I go there, I want to speak of things in my own life.

There was a time that God told me to write a book on homosexuality and what the Bible has to say about it. When God first told me that, I was wondering, why me? I thought that they would certainly try to kill me for going against them like that. But eventually I did it. When I first started out I did a lot of research on it. I had a study Bible and went through the concordance as well.

It took me approx. a year or more to get through with all of the study and research that was involved. This was not the hard part. The hard part was finding enough courage to put it into print. To give you an idea of how long it took me to do this, I wasn't even married when God told what he wanted done. Before I was ready to release it and put it into book form, took another fourteen years to do. In other words, this took a long time. Not because it took this long but it was more a result of my disobedience.

First of all, I was asking myself how was I going to do this? This was not my place to ask how this was going to get done. It would have to be God doing it through me. After all, he was the one that wanted me to do it. Second of all, I started and stopped writing, which also took a lot longer than it had to be. This was a combination of disobedience and fear. God says in **(Jn. 14:15)** "If you love me keep my commandments" (KJV).

Third and finally, I got scared when I was about to finish all of the research because this was no longer going to be just words in a book; but going out there talking and advertising this book so others could read about it as well. So as you can see, not only people in the Bible were doing things wrong and not totally following the Lord, but I did it too.

Now we can go to the New testament. The one I want to start out with first is Zachariah. It says in **(Lu. 1:8-10)** *"And it came to pass, that while he executed the priest's office before God in the order of his course, According to the custom of the priest's office, his lot was to burn incense when he went into the temple of the Lord. And the whole multitude of the people were praying without at the time of incense." (KJV)*

Let's go onto verse **(11)** through **(13)**. So far, things are looking good for John. Then as we go further, in verse **(18)** John begins to doubt what the angel was telling him. This is why I said so far so good, because things are going to get extremely hard for John. As we read further in verses **(19)** through **(20)**, the angel has some very unpleasant things to tell John here. So you see God does not like fear or unbelief. If God said it, our response should be, *"I will do it"*.

Let me try to explain why this was so hard for John. The Bible says that he would be silent and unable to speak. I submit to you that Zechariah was not only death, but he became dumb as well because he could not hear anything and this made it difficult for him to speak. I would also imagine that God closed his mouth as well.

To prove this I want to go to (**Lk. 1:59-64**). Now when it says that he had to use gestures, he never heard what they were talking about, and as a result, didn't know how to tell them anything. Since he was able to write after this happened, this was still a way for him to communicate.

If a person was born death, the only way he would be able to communicate is through sign language. I will not argue with you if you come to another conclusion because it is not worth arguing about. So since the death use sign language, Zechariah had to use the written language.

The second place that this happened is when Jesus told Peter to come out to him in the water and what did Peter do? Let's recap the story a little. Starting in (**Mt. 14:24-26**), Jesus has just come up to them walking on the water when they think he is a ghost. To fully make a decision in Peter's mind if he is a ghost or not, Peter asked him if it was really him, to tell him to come out to Jesus, walking on the water.

Then in verse (**28**) through verse (**30**), Peter can be heard yelling out to Jesus to save him. Then in verse (**31**), Jesus simply asked him where is your faith and why did you doubt? He emphasized it by saying "*Oh ye of little faith*" (**Mt. 14:31b**) (**KJV**).

If Jesus told you to do it, this should have been enough evidence to Peter that he could actually do this. But instead of doing what Jesus told him to do and concentrating on that, he took his eyes off of Jesus, his mind as well because he was looking at the water, and finally as a result of all these things, sank; (**II Tim. 1:7**).

There are times when you can even make decisions that are not in your best interest as far as God is concerned. There are times when you should just be content with what you have and not try to over step your boundaries. This can be found in (**Mt. 20:20**). You see this was their mistake. They should have just been contented to go onto heaven with Jesus after they died. So then Jesus proceeds to ask them a question: (**Mt. 20:22a**) and their response is recorded in verse (**22b**).

Then Jesus continues to answer as to why he asked them this question and to qualify them for his answer in return: verse (**23**). Now when the other disciples heard what these two asked Jesus, they were kind of upset. I guess they were saying to themselves who do these negroes think they are?

Jesus knew that so he had to make things right between all of them again. This is why the Bible records: **(Mt. 20:24-28)**. There is another place which says knowledge puffs up but love builds up or edifies, **(I Cor. 8:1)**; KJV.

With this note, I think this is a good time to recap. So I started out with Adam and how God gave him the responsibility to take and tend the garden and to keep it. In other words, it was his responsibility to protect it from outside influences that would cause death.

The next example I gave consisted of Solomon and what he did with all of his wisdom, knowledge and influence. Instead of doing what God told him to do, he decided to do exactly what both Him and his father told him not to do.

I also gave you examples of why people would leave you alone if they saw that whatever you did was getting you blessed. They will end up doing one of two things. One, they will either love and honor you because they can see that God is all over your life; or they will be jealous of you, like Saul did over David, and got mad and jealous to the point of wanting to kill him. These examples can be found in **(I Sam. 18:6-9)**; and **(10)** through **(12)**.

I even gave you an example out of my life as to how I was told by God to write a book which took me over ten years to write and put out there. But because of fear and disobedience it took a lot longer than it should have.

I hope this sermon has been an eye opening and enjoyable experience. Please take to heart the things that please God and the things that don't. As the Bible says: *"Think on these things"*;

(Ph. 4:8b) (KJV).

My time is up and I thank you for yours!

CHAPTER 2

THE TRIPLE THREAT

Love, joy and peace make up the triple threat. All three help us to deal with our fellowman in a genuine, peaceful and loving manner. The triple threat comes through the conversion process of salvation. The word of God says when you get saved, old things are passed away, behold all things become new according to (II Cor. 5:17) (KJV). We also get the triple threat through a need and desire to help others.

When Scripture says "old things are passed away", this means your life before Christ and salvation has been not only forgiven, but it has also been forgotten by the Father God. This includes all of your past and present sins that you have asked God to forgive you for.

When Paul writes "all things become new", this means you now see things through the eyes of God instead of your sinful ways. In other words, you no longer want to do the things you used to do; like hang out with the people you used to hang out with, get high, do drugs, lust after women and having sex outside of marriage. Instead, you desire to do the things the Holy Spirit desires. This includes going to church, reading your Bible, praying, going to Bible study, and witnessing.

After you get saved, you see things differently. The word of God includes a formula to stay that way. Rom. 12:1-2 states: *"I beseech you therefore, brethren, by the mercies of God that you present your bodies a living sacrifice, holy, acceptable to God, which is your reasonable service."*(KJV). Let's stick a pin there. <u>Beseech</u> is a strong word. It means: (I beg you, implore you, or strongly listen to what I am about to say to you). The next word I want to focus on is <u>mercies</u>. This comes from the Greek word: *oiktirmos* which means to have pity or mercy. So God had pity or showed mercy to us when He saw the state we were in. He wanted to help us live a richer and more prosperous life and not hit hell wide open.

The writer goes on to say to "<u>present your bodies</u>". If you have ever served in the military, there are times when you have to present yourself to your superior officers or enlisted men when it is time for inspection. When they inspect you, they are looking for anything out of place so they can fault you for it. Also, while you are in the military your body is not your own any longer; it belongs to the U.S. Government.

Similarly, when God says to present your bodies, it means to be submissive to whatever the Spirit of God tells you to do. In this case, He wants you to present your bodies "a living sacrifice". This means He wants you to sacrifice yourself in the form of dying to this world spiritually, and begin living for God now. In other words, you must die to everything this world offers that is not consistent with a godly lifestyle.

Gal. 2:20a further illustrates this point. It says: *"I am crucified with Christ: nevertheless I live; yet not I, but Christ liveth in me"* (KJV). When you crucify someone you are killing them physically. Similarly, when the verse says "I have been crucified" this means that he died spiritually and the things that he is and does are no longer him, but it's Christ who now lives in him.

The next word the writer uses is <u>holy</u>. This word in the Greek means sacred, pure, consecrated and a saint. Consecrated means to complete, accomplish, consummate (in character), finish, fulfill, make perfect.

Then the writer uses the word <u>acceptable</u>. This simply means the Father is in agreement and fully pleased. Finally, the writer uses the words, "<u>your reasonable service</u>". This simply means this is the least you can do. In other words, this is not asking too much, but should automatically be expected if you are truly a Christian.

Then the writer goes on to say, *"and be not conformed to this world, but be transformed by the renewing of your mind, that you may prove what is that good and acceptable and perfect will of God."*(Rm. 12:2) (KJV).

When the writer says don't be conformed to this world, it means do not be like this world. In other words, don't do things like the world does. For example, in order to gain wealth and accomplish things, the world will lie and cheat for it. But you are to pray and ask God for things and He will tell you what to do in order to achieve those same goals and use it for His glory.

The next word is <u>transformed</u>. This means to change from the way you were doing things to doing things the way God wants you to.

Then God uses the word renew, which means to change your mind from what it used to do, to what the Word of God tells you to do.

Then the writer points out that "<u>you may prove</u>". This word prove literally means to try, examine or test. In other words, God literally wants you to put Him to the test and try what He is telling you, and see if you come to the same conclusion.

Then the writer uses the words "<u>good, acceptable and perfect will of God</u>". Good can be used for the person who gets up and reads his Bible, prays and goes to church. Acceptable is a person who not only reads his Bible, prays and goes to church, but also witnesses.

The last category is perfect, which means that he not only does the former things that were just mentioned, but finds out from God exactly what He wants him to do and then does it.

Everyone deserves to be treated with love. Love is the only common denominator that distinguishes you as a Christian and as one of His disciples—this is according to (Jn. 13:34-35). Love also covers all sins (Prov. 10:12).

Let's begin with the first verse with the mention of "<u>a new commandment</u>." This new commandment the writer is referring to was not in the original commandments given to Moses on Mount Sinai, which can be found in (Ex. 20:1-17). In one instance, it tells them to love God which is found in (Ex. 20:6). However, it never tells them to love each other which can be found in (Jn. 13:34). If that wasn't the case, the Pharisees and Sadducees would not have wanted Jesus and His apostles killed, as stated in the New Testament.

Then verse(35) goes on to say *"and all will know that you are my disciples if you have love one for another."* (K]JV). A disciple is a learner or pupil according to Strong's Concordance. In other words, you are a student of Jesus Christ. Since you are a student of Jesus Christ, the love you show to others will cover all sins according to (Prov. 10:12). This means if a person is mean to you instead of retaliating, you not only forgive but pray and show love. This will get them thinking and eventually lead to them changing their evil ways.

I have been attacked many times by kids in my neighborhood as a child and adult. In those instances, you have to remember *"when you are attacked or ridiculed for my sake and the gospel, great is your reward in heaven"* (Mt. 5:11-12). Love is the reason God sent His one and only Son to die on the cross so we may have eternal life (Jn. 3:16). Love is the greatest initiator on earth because everything you do or say must have love attached to it (I Cor. 13:1).

In (I Cor. 13:1) it states, *"Though I speak with the tongues of men and of angels, but have not love, I have become as sounding brass or a tingling cymbal."* (KJV). If I don't show love when I speak to people, it is all in vain. It is like I am making noise in God's ears. For example, my family is trying to take over my mother's estate and leave me out, even though I took care of my mother when she was sick and stuck in a hospital bed. I brought her home with me to take care of her. I even took care of her remains when she passed away. Even though my entire family was not involved in that, they still think they deserve access to all of her money and assets. Despite my flesh wanting to wreak havoc on them, God tells me to love them anyway and follow His leading in order to get out of this dilemma.

Joy is another important gift of the Spirit to have as part of your arsenal. This also represents the second threat. There are and will be many times when you might want to give up this Christian walk or get discouraged because of circumstances, situations or trouble. That trouble could come in the form of financial problems, marital difficulties or even trouble with addiction in you or your family members—this is according to (Neh. 8:10b).

Now I know this sounds strange, but the joy of the Lord is a deep sense of love you have towards the Father and your fellowman. This is to keep you connected to Jesus Himself. As you stay connected to Jesus and His strength, then you are connected to His power and not your own. Joy is something that remains when all of the laughter and good things that have happened to you are gone (Ps. 16:11). Essentially when things get rough and you don't know what to do, God will show you which path to take. When you are obedient to the Spirt of God, that is when God will meet you and there will be fullness of joy.

When it says "in your presence", this means you can only get joy from God. Therefore, the devil can never interfere with that. This is why there should be rejoicing because this is telling you no matter what happens to you or your family, His joy will be with you as well as His strength. Another reason why we should be joyful even when hard times come is because of

(Ps. 40:14). God will confuse your foes when they come against you. God will also judge them for you, separate them from you and deal with them to the point that they are powerless to do anything to you because of the power of the living God.

Peace, which is the third part of the triple threat, is another attribute you must have as a Christian in order to stay calm even when the waves of life come and try to drag you under. I remember a time when I parked my car outside an apartment complex to deliver something to someone. As I went into the building and up the elevator, I remembered I had forgotten to lock the door. Not only that, but my car was also running. In my mind I just knew that my car would be gone when I got out of there. Before I left the apartment complex, and I was there for several minutes, I said a quick prayer to God asking Him to watch over my car.

When I got back outside, my car was still there, running and untouched. This is because

(Mk. 11:24) states: *"Therefore I say unto you, What things soever ye desire, when ye pray, believe that ye receive them, and ye shall have them."* (KJV) This is God's Word and it will not come back to Him void (Is. 55:11); and this can also be illustrated by another Scripture

(Num. 23:19).

In Is. 55:11 it states: *"when that word comes out of His mouth, it will not come back to him void"*. This means that it will not come out of His mouth without power or purpose. It also means that nothing or no one can stop this from happening. The next part says: *"It will accomplish what I please, and it will prosper in the thing for which I sent it."* God's Word will do exactly what it was intended to do. For example, there is a verse which says, *"Whatsoever you bind on earth will be bound in heaven,"* (Mt. 18:18a). If the devil is trying to unleash hell in your life, you have the right to bind him through the name of Jesus, and God will run to your rescue in order to make sure this happens. The Word continues, *"It will prosper in the thing for which I sent it."* Prosper means it will grow in power and dominion where everyone can see, and will do exactly what the word you are using is designed to do.

The Word of God says: *"God will keep you in perfect peace whose mind is stayed on thee because he trusts in thee"* (Is. 26:3). Therefore, if you say you trust in God but have no peace, you are being fooled by the devil. If God's Word says it, that is all that needs to be said. You must also be convinced that if God be for you, who can be against you (Rom. 8-31b). God is the strongest force in the universe. No one is as great as He. So if God is on your side, no one in the earth, underneath the earth, or in the spiritual realm can defeat you.

This is like having martial arts fighter Bruce Lee on your side when you are dealing with your enemies and they want to start a fight. I guarantee they will run when they find out Bruce Lee will be right alongside you fighting. This is exactly what it is like to have God fighting for you especially since God has never lost a battle.

I know this all sounds well and good, but the Lord will test you and the devil will tempt you into doing something that has the potential of taking you further from the will and Word of God. I spent a lot of time in a former ministry. I did everything the minister taught. The test came when the minister told me to give more money than I gave in order for God to bless me. He used the Bible verse about when God came to Solomon after he had sacrificed the cattle and sheep, and asked him what do you want me to do for you (I Ki. 3:4-5). I found out later on that God didn't even want me in that ministry. Furthermore, He had not sanctioned me to give all of that money I gave to him. This caused hostility in my household and a strain to my bank account. So, the devil took that opportunity to trick me and God was testing me to see which way I was going to go.

The peace came when I listened to the Holy Spirit and went to the church that He wanted me to go to and became a member of the church he wanted me to be at. After I went to this new church, Friendly Temple

Church of God in Christ, my mind was relieved of my past mistakes and peace came by being obedient to the Spirit of the Lord.

Don't get it twisted. God always gives you a choice. He gave it to Adam and Eve regarding the tree of the knowledge of good and evil (Gen. 2:16-17). He gave it to Cain when he got mad at God for not honoring his offering, but accepting Abel's instead (Gen. 4:3-7). He gave a choice to Abram and Sarai when God told Abram he would have a son at the appointed time (Gen. 15:2-4). This took ten years to happen. Since it took so long in their eyes, Sarai told Abram to go into her handmaiden and have a child. This union produced Ishmael who was not the son of the promise. This is the very reason why the Middle East is having such a hard time to this day (Gen. 16:1-4,11; Gen. 17:17-19). He also gave it to David when he counted all of the nation of Israel after God told him not to do it and judged him for it (I Chron. 21:1-8). Be careful to listen to the Holy Spirit before you make a decision. If you don't, it could be the wrong one. And if it is, you will pay the consequences for it.

Now to recap, love is the first thing you should have when dealing with the triple threat. Whatever you do must be done in love or you are like "sounding brass or a tingling cymbal" as noted in (I Cor. 13:1). To stay that way, you must incorporate (Rm. 12:1-2) which states: *"I beseech you therefore brethren by the mercies of God that you present your bodies a living sacrifice which is your reasonable service."* (KJV).

Then there is joy. If you can remember nothing else, remember that "the joy of the Lord is your strength" (Neh. 8:10b) (KJV). (Ps. 40:14) states: *"Let them be ashamed and confounded together that seek after my soul to destroy it; let them be driven backward and put to shame that wish me evil."* (KJV). Do you remember what I said this meant? It means God will confuse your foes when they come against you. God will also judge them for you, separate them from you, and deal with them to the point that they are powerless to do anything to you because of the power of the living God.

And finally we come to (Is. 26:3) which says: *"Thou shall keep you in perfect peace whose mind is stayed on thee because he trusts in thee."* (KJV). Then (Rm. 8:31b) states: *"If God be for you who can be against you"* (KJV). God is the strongest force in the universe and if He is fighting your battles, no one stands a chance no matter who they are.

CHAPTER 3

WHY EVERYONE NEEDS
A COVERING

This particular sermon is going to be dealing with coverings, which refers to a person's need to answer to a force or entity greater than himself. In this case, the force or entity that will be discussed is the Father God, who is the covering for us all. Within this sermon, I will cover why we need a covering, who is covered, and how this covering can protect you from whatever physical or spiritual force is out there.

According to (Job 22:14), the word covering is taken from the Hebrew word *cathar* which means something that hides you (either good or bad), conceals, keeps close, or keeps a secret. Another version of that same word is *cether* which means the same thing but is more related to how someone is able to protect you. This version of the Hebrew word is more related with how God is able to protect you (Deut. 32).

When I was growing up in Boston, there were times when I would have problems with some of the kids. So, I would either call on my father or brother to help. Just the mere appearance of them showing their faces would cause all of the kids to turn and run. This is exactly how God wants to protect you. When you allow Him to show up in your life, and you learn to speak the word to make the devil flee, you become a force to be reckoned with. One of those words is *"Submit yourselves therefore to God; resist the devil and he will flee from you."* (Jm. 4:7 KJV)

For example, let's say you don't understand something about the Word of God. You can either go to a close friend who is adept at the Word to help you figure it out; or you can go to a pastor or other religious leader to see what he has to say; or you can study that topic for yourself to get the interpretation from God Himself. Whatever way you choose, God can use that experience to get out of it exactly what He wants you to see.

There was a time when I could not understand the word found in (I Jn. 4:18) which says: *"There is no fear in love; but perfect love casteth out fear."* (KJV). I would ask God what that meant because I could not understand for the life of me how a person could go through life and not be afraid of anything. Then God told me to pray every time I read my Bible. This went on for some time. It seemed that day after day I could not get certain fears out of my life.

As I continued to pray over this before I read my Bible, there were certain situations that became a lot easier to do. One of those fears was driving at night. It seemed that the more I was called on to drive after the sun went down, it was hard at first. Then as I continued to pray over it like God told me to, I suddenly didn't seem to care if it was night or day. As this went on for some time, it suddenly dawned on me that God had finally taken that fear away from me. This continued to happen over and over again in different areas of my life.

(Deut. 32:1-10), illustrates how God has looked over the whole world, as well as the heavens and everything else in between, in order to provide order to His creation. With regard to the nation of Israel in particular (Deut. 32:10) says God has kept Jacob as "the apple of His eye" (KJV). So, what this is essentially saying is everyone needs someone to confide in every once in a while. This is normally when trials or questions come or you need some moral support. God is saying He is there to give all of that and more.

Now let's break this down Scripture by Scripture so we can see what this is telling us. Deut. 32:1 says: *"Give ear, O heavens, and I will speak and hear, O earth, the words of my mouth"*. God is starting out with the heavens that He created back in (Gen. 1:). God spoke everything that exists in the earth by His mouth according to (Gen. 1:3; 1:6; 1:9).

God goes on to say in (Deut. 32:2), *"Let my teaching drop as the rain; My speech settles as the dew, as raindrops on the tender herb, and as showers on the grass"*. These things God is referring to happen over and over again during certain times of the year. In other words, as much as it rains or the dew comes down on the earth, is the amount of time God speaks to us about us and what we need to do in order to become more like Him.

In Rm. 1:19 (NLT) it says, *"They know the truth about God because he has made it obvious to them. For ever since the world was created, people have seen the earth and sky. Through everything God made, they can clearly see his invisible qualities his eternal power and divine nature. So, they have no excuse for not knowing God."* Everywhere you turn your eyes to look, there is another force that did all of this—that force is God. This is why God says before you take a step or make a decision, consult Him first.

Let's start out with this body we are in. *"What? Know ye not that your body is the temple of the Holy Ghost which is in you that you have of God and you are not your own? For you are bought with a price. Therefore, glorify God in your body and in your spirit, which are God's"* (I Cor. 6:19) (KJV). God is a covering for your body so you can't do anything you want with it. When Jesus died on the cross, He died for you to have the ability to live inside your body free from sin which will take you to hell.

(Prov. 3:5-6) says: *"Trust in the Lord with all of thine heart. And Lean not to thine own understanding. In all thy ways acknowledge him and he shall direct thy paths."* (KJV). You can't even make up your own mind without consulting God in terms of where to worship, who to marry, or where you should even go to school for higher education. All of these decisions are important and will either put you in a position to have positive success or more problems with the wrong ones. These are just a few concerns we will have as we go through this thing called life.

Let's say you are in a car and someone cuts in front of you causing you to almost get into a serious accident. When you call out the name of Jesus, God dispatches angels on your behalf that can prevent this from happening. For example, I was around ten years old when I was riding my bike down a street that became a dangerous hill. My speed increased the further down the hill I went. To make matters worse, my pant leg got caught in the bike chain. Back in those days, the only way you could stop a bike was with the foot brake. Without the ability to brake the situation became increasingly dangerous. After I got down so far, I called out the name of Jesus and said a prayer that I would not be killed or hurt. When I did this, I ended up turning down a steep driveway that was steeper than the street I was coming down. By some supernatural force, I was able to turn around in that driveway without a scratch. My friends who were there and saw what happened wanted to know how I did this. I didn't have any idea at the time. But in retrospect, I know it was God sending His angel to help me survive that incident. This is an example of the covering God has over us.

A similar incident happened to Gideon in the Bible. In Judges, Gideon was facing possible defeat from his enemies, but God gave him a way out (Judg. 7:9-15). God delivered him out of that situation as He has done so many times with so many different people both in the Bible as well as now.

God is also a covering for pastors as well as anyone in the church. The pastor should be the covering of parishioners. In large churches, God has helps in place such as assistant pastors, elders, and ministers who can provide guidance in the event the pastor can't be there himself. We see this example of helps in (Ex. 18:14-23) where Moses' father-in-law Jethro came to see what he was doing. The task of dealing with all the people was too big for Moses so Jethro gave him a solution to follow so he would not be worn out.

Jesus was driven out to the desert by the Spirit (Mt. 4:1). This was Jesus' Fathers' Spirit compelling Him to go into the desert to be tempted by the devil. Jesus had no choice in the matter. Therefore, it was not Him making that decision but His Father in Heaven. This is indicative of the fact that God was Jesus's covering. Jesus also made a statement that whatever He heard the Father speak He spoke (Jn. 7:16). There are times I have heard Pastor Thomas say he had one sermon ready to deliver but God changed it and told him to speak on another subject instead. I have even heard Assistant Pastor Cory say he was prepared to speak on one subject, but God changed it so he could speak to a woman who was considering taking her life. That is how God can be a covering for a pastor.

Time will not allow me to go into all of the possible instances that a covering is present, but these are the most popular ways God can set up coverings for you or someone else in the church including the pastor. As I stated, even Jesus had a covering, Jesus was also a covering for His disciples. Whenever the Pharisees would ask them a question about something, Jesus was the one to answer it (Mk. 2:15-17).

It has been a pleasure going through the different ways God and others can be a covering in the church and over others' lives. Whenever God speaks through the pastor, evangelist, teacher, or prophet, this is God speaking to you and at that moment God is allowing this person to be a covering over you because he is giving you sound advice from the throne room of God.

CHAPTER 4

WHY WE NEED TO STAY CLOSE TO JESUS CHRIST

G od is the reason: *"For in Him we live, and move, and have our being* (Acts 17:28) (KJV). For the next few moments, I am going to break down this Scripture and tell you what it means. Let me start this sermon by saying that Christ means anointed one or Messiah. The word live in the Greek means to be saved from death, to be alive, or to preserve. When Jesus Christ gave His life on the cross, He saved us from dying because we were headed to hell (Ps. 9:17). God promised we would have life and that more abundantly (Jn. 10:10). If you follow God's Word as well as believe in the Lord Jesus Christ, you shall have life.

There was a certain rich man who came to Jesus wanting to know how he could have eternal life (Mt. 19:16). Jesus told him to keep the commandments (Mt. 19:17). This man had done all of these things from his youth (Mt. 19:20). Then Jesus told him if you want to be perfect, which in the Greek is *teleios*, (meaning to be complete, in character, consecrate, finish, fulfil, make perfect) If thou wilt be perfect, go and sell what thou hast, and give to the poor, and thou shalt haver treasure in heaven: and come and follow me." (Mt. 19:21) (KJV). But when the young man heard that saying, he went away sorrowful: for he had great possessions." (Mt. 19:22) (KJV).

If you want to be close to the Lord, you cannot have any distractions that take you away from serving the Lord or following Him. This man's money was a distraction. That is why Jesus told him to get rid of it because with it he could never be mature in Christ. Jesus said, *"I am the way, the truth and the life"* (Jn. 14:6) (KJV), and in another place Jesus said: *"I am the resurrection and the life" (Jn. 11:25)* (KJV). Therefore, when you are in Christ you will have life.

Even Peter was distracted in following Jesus. Jesus had just been resurrected from the dead and had appeared to His disciples (Jn. 21:12). Before this, three times Peter denied he knew God (Mt. 26:31-34). Even though Peter said this, that is exactly what he did. Therefore, there was no time for him to be scared (II Tim. 1:7). As he was on the shore eating and talking with His disciples, Jesus asked Peter if he loved Him (Jn. 21:15). Peter answered him "yes Lord" and He told him to feed His lambs. Then He asked him a second time, "Peter do you love me?" and Peter said once again, "Lord you know that I love you." Then He told Peter to tend to His sheep (Jn. 21:16). Finally, a third time Jesus asked Peter if He loved Him and once again Peter said the same thing and Jesus told him to feed His sheep (Jn. 21:17). Jesus asked Peter three times if he loved Him because He wanted to reinforce in Peter what he was here to do. Since he was called to be an Apostle (Mt. 10:2), his assignment was to feed Jesus's sheep with the Word of God (Acts 2:12-21).

In Acts 2, there were 120 people in the upper room waiting to be filled with the Holy Spirit. When the Spirit finally did settle on them, they all began to speak in tongues in all of the languages of that region. After this happened, the people thought they were drunk with wine. This is what caused Peter to point out that the people were not drunk.

Finally, Peter was called to be a pillar in the church of the Lord Jesus Christ which Jesus had just died for (Mt. 16:13-18). To prove this, Peter is the only person in the New Testament who God allowed to speak to two people in the church who were trying to defile the church of the Lord Jesus Christ by lying to the Holy Spirit or God (Acts 5:1-5). When it says that all fear came across all who heard it, this meant that God was letting the people know that He would not allow this to happen. This was critical because if the church was to prosper and grow, people had to develop a fear of the Lord and bind Satan.

Then slipping down to Jn. 21:20, Peter turned around, saw the disciple whom Jesus loved following, and asked Jesus "what about this man?" This man happened to be John. Then Jesus said to him *"If I will that he remains or live until I come back, what is that to you? You follow me"* (Jn. 21:22). This is a good word to all of us: do not worry about someone else. You do what God has specifically called you to do. When you worry about someone else, that stops you from being all God called you to be. This is found in (2 Cor. 10:12), and alluded to in (Col. 4:17). This ministry the Word is referring to is the work or assignment that God gave you to do in His name.

The second word I want to deal with is move. When someone moves, that means that he is not standing still. He is doing something. Move in the Greek means just that—to move or go. Jesus sent out His disciples to witness to the people, and to heal the sick (Lk. 9:1-2). Ananias was sent to Saul who later became Paul so he could receive his sight and become a Christian (Acts 9:10-11, 17). Philip was sent to an Ethiopian eunuch to witness to him (Acts 8:26-30; 31-33); this is taken from (Isaiah 53). Then continuing in the Scriptures (Acts 8:34-39), Jesus was often moved in the Spirit to heal someone (Mk. 1:41, Jn. 9:1-7). He even promised the same thing to us (Jn. 14:12).

The final word I want to deal with is being. In the Greek, it means it is I or act of being. What this is saying is who you really are. The dictionary says this word means: a living creature, the state or act of existence, consciousness, or life, or something in such a state. My personal favorite is: one's basic nature, or the qualities thereof; essence or personality.

What we are as believers is Christians. This word means Christlike. This means that whatever we have read about Jesus doing, we should be doing the same.

CHAPTER 5

THE DEATH BURIAL AND RESURRECTION OF JESUS

Many times Jesus told His disciples He would be accused by the religious leaders, as well as the Pharisees and Sadducees. As a result, He would be crucified, buried, but on the third day would be raised from the dead.

Let's start with the first thing mentioned which was Jesus telling His disciples He would be accused of blasphemy, which was the main reason the Jews believed Jesus should be crucified. The first place this is mentioned is in (Mk. 2:2b-7). Another important point to mention is when Jesus responded to the Jews concerning Abraham. Jesus had been telling the Jews and religious leaders that Abraham looked forward to His coming and was very happy (Jn. 8:56). Then the next point that should be made is absolutely priceless. This is when Jesus told the Jews that before Abraham was I am (Jn. 8:56-58). Right after Jesus told them that they wanted to kill Him (Jn. 8:59).

This is all a precursor to Jesus actually being put to death through crucifixion. This is going to begin with a mock trial. It should also be mentioned that the high priest prophesied that Jesus would not only die for the Jews but for the whole nation—that being the nation of believers who would believe on His name after He was raised from the dead (Jn. 11:49-52).

I want to give one instance where Jesus alludes to the fact that He would be crucified because He tells His disciples He would be raised from the dead (Mt. 17:9). Now to comment on a time when Jesus told His disciples straight out that He would be betrayed and killed, but raised from the dead on the third day (Mt. 17:22-23).

Before we go to the mock trial, we can't forget about Judas who made this all possible. Jesus had always been telling them through the Holy Spirit that someone would betray Him and all of them were not clean. One of those occasions was when Jesus decided to wash His disciple's feet (Jn. 13:10-11). Judas finds out the Pharisees wanted to kill Jesus and begins to plot how to deliver Jesus to His enemies (Mk. 14:10-11). The Pharisees decided this also had to be done in secret because they did not want to risk a riot breaking out (Mt. 26:3-5).

Finally, let's begin to talk about the mock trial as I mentioned before. The law said at least two or three witnesses were needed in order to put someone to death or for something to be proven true (Jn. 8:17). The thought behind this is if just one person says that he did it, that person could be lying. But if you have at least two witnesses, it is more likely to be true. This was the case involving Jesus. In (Mt. 26:57), Jesus is taken into the high priest's headquarters to be questioned.

First he asked Jesus what He was teaching the people. Jn. 18:20 was Jesus's reply. Then

(Mt. 26:59-62) was the time when two people got up and said *"this man said I am able to destroy the temple and build it up in three days."* (NLT)

The final charge came when the high priest asked Jesus if He was the Messiah, the Son of God. Jesus replied: *"You have said it. And in the future you will see the Son of Man seated in the place of power at God's right hand and coming on the clouds of heaven."* After hearing what Jesus said about Himself, all the people present at the trial wanted Him crucified for blasphemy (Mt. 26:65-66).

After it was agreed that Jesus should be crucified for blasphemy, He had to be brought out to the town called Golgotha, which means "the place of the skull" (Mt. 27:32-35 NLT). This was just the beginning. Finally in (Mt. 27:45-50), Jesus dies and gives up the Ghost after they offered Him sour wine.

Now we come to the best part—the resurrection. In (Jn. 20:1-9), the first person Jesus revealed Himself to after the resurrection was Mary Magdalene (Jn. 20:11-12). Now skipping down to verse (14), as Mary thought on this, she was about to leave when she saw someone in front of her thinking that it was the gardener, and asked him where have you laid the body of Jesus so I can get Him (Jn. 20:15-16).

Jesus then revealed Himself to some of the other disciples (Jn. 20:19-23). However, Thomas was not there so when they told him they had seen Jesus, he did not want to believe it.

Therefore, Jesus had to appear to him in person so he would no longer be faithless but believe (Jn. 20:24-27). This next part is my favorite. This is after Thomas had seen Jesus and finally believes. This is found in (Jn. 20:28-29).

I hope this has been a good presentation of how Jesus was betrayed, put on trial, found guilty of blasphemy, crucified, and finally resurrected from the dead so as to be seen by others as well as His disciples.

THE BATTLE IS STILL ON

There is a battle still on just in case you didn't know it. That is why Paul told us in (**Eph. 6:10-18**), to put on the whole armor of God. Why do you need armor on for unless you are about to go into battle, or the battle is already on? Another interesting thing about the scriptures I just mentioned is that, the Word tells us to put it on but never ever does it tell us to take it off. Therefore, the battle continues to rage.

Now I would like to go step by step through these scriptures I just mentioned, to make sure that there is no confusion about them. First of all, the word says in (**Eph. 6:10**), that this is a <u>final word</u>. When Paul says this, it means that this is the final word as far as this book of the Bible is concerned. It can also be interpreted that this is the final word Paul has to say on the subject of spiritual warfare. After all, this is the last chapter in Ephesians. Then Paul writes, be strong in the Lord and in his mighty power, or the power of his might.

Right off the back, you should come to the conclusion that this is not your power but Gods'. God is the one that has all power in his hands, (**Is. 41:10**); *"Don't be afraid, for I am with you. Don't be discouraged, for I am your God. I will strengthen you and help you. I will hold you up with my victorious right hand"* (NLT).

First of all, God is telling us not to be afraid in, (**Is. 41:1**). Why is God saying that? Because he says that the fight is not yours but the Lords'; (**II Chron. 20:15**). So if the battle is the Lords' then what do you have to fear. There is another word that says in: (**Rm. 8:31**), *"What shall we say then to these things? If God be for us who can be against us?* " (KJV). There is also a word in: (**II Tim. 1:7**), also telling us not to fear and also tells us why.

Then in verse (**Eph. 6:11a**), it says to: *"Put on all of Gods armor."* (NLT). Obviously, when it says all of Gods armor, you are not to miss anything. Later on we will tell you what makes up the armor of God. For right now it tells us not to miss anything. In other words, don't forget to put anything on.

Let's use an example from a sport that we all know about. That is the sport of football. There are a lot of things that make up the uniform of a football player; that if you miss anything, this could result in you being seriously hurt. You have a helmet to protect your head, shoulder pads to protect your shoulders and neck, knee pads to protect you when you fall and a cup that protects your privates. With all of these protective equipment that is used, all help to keep the football player safe from serious injury.

Similarly, this is what the armor of God is supposed to do. Now that you have all of God's armor on, what are you supposed to do now? The word tells us "*it will help you to stand firm from all of the strategies of the devil*". The devil is the arch enemy of the Christian. This is because the devil, before he was known as the devil or satan, was a glorious angel: (**Is. 14:12-17**). In addition to this, his name was Lucifer, (**Is. 14:12**), in the (KJV).

Now going to verse (**12**), the word tells us what we are not fighting. But this is one of the areas that the devil uses against God's people to fool us. Currently, and for many years since we have been in this country and before, we have been fighting someone. But to be absolutely accurate, none of them have been against other people, even though it may have seemed like that. But that is what the devil wants you to think. The reason why he likes it like this is because the more we fight against ourselves, the less we will fight against the devil himself. However, the word tells us exactly what we are fighting. That being: "*evil rulers and authorities of the unseen world, and against evil spirits in high places*", the (KJV), says. The (NLV) tells us in heavenly places. But I like high places better than heavenly places.

It was already covered how he came out of heaven trying to be God or just like him. After all, God made Lucifer, who later on became satan rather than the other way around. Also, even Jesus made mention of the devil when he used the reference of *lightening* in, (**Lu. 10:18**) (KJV).

Going further on in that same verse, it goes on to say; *evil rulers of the unseen world*. This is to indicate that the spirit world is more real than the physical world. After all, think of 9-11. There were the twin towers that stood powerful and strong to indicate strength, beauty, and excellence. But when that unforeseen day happened, those twin towers that were there became not. In other words, they were no longer there. This plane coming out of nowhere hit it dead on.

Then when it says: *mighty powers in this dark world;* what this is telling us is that if you are not filled with the Spirit, that being, the Spirit of God, it would be impossible for you to defeat the devil's weapons. This is where this armor comes in. Also it says in dark places. This means that the devil cannot be seen with human eyes. It can only be seen in the spirit realm.

There is a story about Elisha, in 2 Kings that the Bible refers to when discussing this story. It is found in **(II Ki. 6:11-17)**. Just like the servant of Elisha couldn't see these angels before Elisha prayed for him, is the same way that you without the Spirit of God, can't see the devil and his demons without the Spirit of the Lord opening up your eyes.

This gift is explained in **(I Cor. 12:10)**. The word uses *discerning of spirits* (KJV). These spirits can be from the Father God, or they can come from the devil himself or from your spirit as well. Either way it goes, you will no longer be in darkness when looking into the spirit world. Then it finally goes on to say spiritual wickedness in high places.

What this is essentially saying is that there are different levels to the devil's power. There are powerful demons, similar to the ones that was in this man called Legion, **(Mk. 5:9)**. These demons were so strong that no human force was able to contain it or restrain it. Then you have small imp demons that are not as powerful as others. I believe one of the strongest demons is the one that is over pornography. Almost every element of our society is being impacted by this demon. These are just some of the weapons that the devil uses at his disposal, to confront Christians as well as non-Christians alike. If it is not pornography itself, it is some sort of topic associated with that subject.

Then we come to verse **(13)**, which says: *"Wherefore take unto you the whole armor of God that you may be able to withstand in the evil day, and having done all, to stand"* (KJV). So to break down this passage of scripture, I would start by saying that Paul reiterates once again about putting on the whole armor of God. Paul likes to emphasize this because it is so important. You can't possible stand without that armor that Ephesians talks about.

When the word says in the *evil day*, this means that when things really begin to get tough, you still have to stand or stand guard over your mind and soul. You do this by using the word of God or remembering what the word of God has to say about your particular situation. For example, when Jesus had to go through the wilderness experience found in **(Mt. 4:1-10)**, verse **(11)**, goes on to say that the devil left him and he was ministered by the angels. This means that Jesus had a hell of a time fighting the devil while in that state of need. That need was eating food once again. As you know, Jesus had to fast for (40) days and (40) nights. Then the Bible says that he was very hungry, (**Mt. 4:2**). But after all of that occurred, he was finally able to eat once again, and on top of that, the angels gave him further peace.

Just imagine if you were in a battle with someone and you hadn't eaten in (40) days. What kind of condition would you be in? Would you be ready for the battle? More to the point, would you even have the energy to fight off anything?

Let's say that you have to run a marathon, and you have had nothing to eat that whole day and maybe in the last few days. Would you be ready to run that 42.2 miles of pavement? This in and of itself would seem like an impossible task. It would be very similar to fighting King Kong. That would also be an impossible task. In other words, it would be like fighting the devil on your own strength. That is impossible too. This is what Jesus had to put up with. So for him, this was his *evil day*.

In other words, when something really bad happens to you, and it is the result of the devil, this is your *evil day*. This could come in a variety of ways. You could catch this virus, you could get robbed, or maybe you lost your house or car keys. This is your *evil day*.

Finally, at the end of verse (**Eph. 6:13**), it says: *"and having done all to stand"* (KJV). This means that as you are going through your *evil day* experience, you are crying out to the Lord, reciting scripture like Jesus did to the devil and even calling out to Christian friends. But even though you are doing all these things, negative stuff is still going on in your life. As it was for Jesus, it will be for you too.

Remember that Jesus had already fasted for (40) days and was very hungry, the word of God says. The word does not tell us how long Jesus had to go through this period of testing. But it had to be over a month. This means that you can be doing all of the right things, but bad things will still continue to happen.

Another example of this can be found in Paul's life. Even though Paul was teaching the word of God to the Jews as well as the Gentiles, he was still being attacked on every side; (**II Cor. 11:22-27**). These were Paul's *evil days*. So just because you are a Christian, or pray, or speak scripture to the devil, or even speak in tongues, sometimes this will not stop the onslaught of negative activity. But what I will tell you is that no matter what the devil does, the true Christian of God will always come out on top.

I would like to use a personal example out of my own life. One day my wife was coming out of the driveway, and going down the street, when this other car came backing out of his driveway and hit the car. Obviously, this was an *evil day* that the devil brought on to discourage us.

At first, we were upset. I was wondering that out of all the times we have been coming down that road, nothing bad has ever happened to us. Now one day this happens. On top of that, we were coming around this corner when this guy that hit the car smiled at me. It was like he was glad that this happened to me

As time went on, I had to take my car down to get it fixed. But God made it all better because for the mere fact that he had no insurance at the time of the accident, I had no deductible to pay. On top of that, I had a car that I was driving around in as if it were my own, from a rent a car agency.

I could hardly wait to drive by his house and allow him to see the new car that I was now driving. This car was in some ways better than my own. This is even backed up in scripture; it is found in (**Ps. 23:5a**). Like I said before, you will always come out on *top*.

Now we get to verse (**Eph. 6:14**), which says: *"Stand therefore, having your loins girt about with truth"* (KJV). Now that is not the end of the scripture in (**14**), but I want to talk a little about what this scripture is saying to the believer. First it says from the end of (13) that *"and having done all to stand"* (KJV); this new scripture in (**14**), is saying to stand again. If you have been keeping count, or even if you haven't, the number of times that these scriptures have the word *stand* in it is a total of (4) times.

The next few verses will be coming from the (NLT) version of the Bible. I like it this way because it is easier to understand what the Word of God is saying to us.

Now after it says *"Stand your ground"*; the next phrase says: *"putting on the belt of truth"*. I am stopping here because this is something very important that needs to be discussed. The word truth, is the very essence of who God is. Jesus said in (**Jn. 14:6**): *"I am the way, the truth, and the life"* (KJV). This resembles what the essence of who the Spirit of God truly is. Then we have the scriptures that says in **(Jn. 4:24)**, *"God is a Spirit, so those who worship him must worship him in Spirit and in truth (KJV)."*

The last one I want to use is found in **(Jn. 8:32)**, which says: *"And ye shall know the truth, and the truth shall make you free;"* (KJV). As I stated in the scriptures; according to: **(Mt. 18:16b)**, "that in the mouth of two or three witnesses, every word may be established;" (KJV). To illustrate this, I have just given you three scripture references of the word truth, as it relates to Gods' personality.

Now this scripture also uses the word loins. This is a Greek word called "osphus", which means hip area and also the genital area. This is where procreative power comes from. So in other words, this is designed to protect the most sensitive and vulnerable areas of your entire body. The whole reason why man was created was to plant a seed and thereby help bring into the world a life that is taught the truth. In this way, when this person grows up, he or she lives and speaks the truth from what he or she was taught.

The next part of this verse says: *"and having on the breastplate of righteousness".* This breastplate that the word is talking about here protects your heart, lungs and a portion of your midsection. This is also another very vital part of your armor as well.

The Greek word for righteousness is: dikaios. This means, you are strong in character. This word character is another interesting word. Character is what and how you act when no one is around to see what you are doing. In other words, anyone can act like they are righteous for a little while others can see them. But will they do those same things in the privacy of their own home when no one else is there but them?

To continue on with the definition of this word dikaios, by implication you are now innocent. In other words, it is like you never sinned. That is because Jesus paid your debt to the Lord; **(Jn. 3:16)**. You also act holy. This means that whatever you see Jesus doing, you must follow suit. This is what makes you holy. This word literally means *set apart*. What are you being set apart for? Of course it is for doing the Lords' will. The word of God also says in

(Lev. 11:45b), *Ye shall therefore be holy for I am holy,* (KJV).

. . . .

Now we come to verse **(Eph. 6:15)**, which says: *"And your feet shod with the preparation of the gospel of peace, (KJV)"* What this is saying is that you have to walk somewhere in order to find someone to talk to about the Son of God. Back in that day, that is all they did back then. They sure didn't have any cars, jets, motorcycles, or buses. For the most part, they either used a donkey, mule, or walked.

The only time I remember Jesus riding anywhere was when he came into Jerusalem riding on a mule; **(Mt. 21:1-11)**. So as I said before, he walked most of the time. Then it is hard to talk to someone about the Lord if you are riding on a mule if the other person is walking. You would have to stop the ass anyway, get off in order to talk to him.

I might also add that Jesus, when He got on that mule, was the first one to ever ride that mule. The reason why I say that is according to **(Mt. 21:2)**; which says: *"Go into the village over there, He said. As soon as you enter it, you will see a donkey tied there, with its colt beside it. Untie them and bring them to me;"* (NLT).

This means that the mule or donkey was young and the colt was even younger because it was the donkey's off spring. Then **(Jn. 12:14-15)**, says: *"Jesus found a young donkey and rode on it, fulfilling the prophecy that said:*

"Don't be afraid, people of Jerusalem. Look, your King is coming, riding on a donkey's colt; (NLT). That is like having a brand-new car in today's standards. Matthew is the one that records the mule and a colt of a mule. A colt is a baby mule.

When the word of God says *"shod"*, this is another word that means to put on. So besides putting on your sandals, you also put on the _gospel of peace_. This means that anywhere you go or might be at, the number one thing on your mind is to bring _peace_ with you as you walk along.

For example, I happened to be in the line of a store. There was a woman behind me and I happened to ask her how was she doing? She told me fine. Then I believe she asked how was I doing. I told her very good because I know the savior; Jesus Christ. Then I proceeded to minister to her about how good He is.

As I was talking to her, I could see her eyes getting really bright and wide. She really liked what I was talking to her about. There was another woman that I was talking to on the phone that is a Muslim. With this in mind, the last thing I told her was that I hoped she would accept the

Lord as her personal savior. Then I told her Shalom. Of course they did not have stores like us back then, but this is the way we put on our feet the gospel of peace.

In **(Eph. 6:16)**, this contains one of the most important parts of your armor that has to be put on. That is faith. God said: "But without faith it is impossible to please him", (Heb. 11:6) (KJV). Why, because God exists in the spirit world and we exist in the physical world. We cannot see God with our natural eyes, so therefore, we have to depend on our spiritual eyes to know that he exists.

The Bible says that *"Faith is the substance of things hoped for, the evidence of things not seen*; (Heb. 11:1) (KJV). This means that you have to believe you already have it in the spirit realm before it becomes visible in the natural. It is not genuine faith at all if you only believe you have it when you see it with your natural eyes. The devil is in the spirit realm as well and knows when God is trying to get something to you. This is when your faith has to be just that much stronger or you may never get it.

That same verse goes on to say that you have to quench all of the fiery darts of the wicked one. This is when the devil begins to put things into your mind to trip you up. The devil will say things like you will never get that because you are not worthy of God giving that to you. He even may try to stop it by getting you to sin in some way. You have to understand that whenever you sin, this short circuits your faith.

What I mean is that the devil will have more power and influence over your thoughts. The devil will say everything in the book about why you will not get this thing you have been waiting for or asking for a bill to be paid on time or you may lose your house.

I hope that this has been a profitable sermon. One in which you can study out for yourself. My time is up and I thank you for yours.

Printed in the United States
By Bookmasters